LOVE FLEW DOWN IN SONG

PATRICIA ANN

Love Flew Down in Song
Copyright © 2021 by Patricia Ann

Tellwell Talent
www.tellwell.ca

ISBN
978-0-2288-5007-6 (Paperback)
978-0-2288-5006-9 (eBook)

Table of Contents

By Patricia Ann

DEDICATION

I dedicate this book to anyone who has suffered within their hearts or is currently suffering from loneliness, depression, health, anxiety, or just being unsure of their place on this Earth and knowing what the Lord wants you to do with your life. Our journeys are unique, and God has a place and a purpose for each of us.

He sent me these songs when I was at some of these dark places in my journey, and if only one of them touches you in your dark time, then I believe I have had a great purpose set before me. I could not hold these words within just for me. My prayer is you will pass them on to another soul who is searching. Thanks be to God.

Amen

INTRODUCTION

God has been sending me songs since I was about fourteen years old. I wouldn't say there are a lot of them compared to other songwriters after this many years have gone by, but that isn't important. They were sent to me when I most needed them. Sometimes, I struggled with everyday life situations, such as being a Christian teenager in a highly secular world of unbelief in my values. I went through a divorce and having two very young children to raise alone. I battled depression with *Seasonal Affective Disorder* (SAD), sometimes for no particular reason at all. Often, I was unsure of what my purpose was living on this Earth God put me on. How could little ol' me make a difference in this world or help bring people closer to God?

I'm sure this is a struggle many of us deal with from time to time on our life's journey. I hope to open people's eyes to be at peace with themselves and one another, to feel fulfilled and content.

God has given me many testimonies, proving to me that He is here for me and in my human weakness, I dare say I need to be reminded more often than not.

It is a very good thing that God has neverending patience with us and loves us unconditionally.

Some songs God brought to me while I was driving in the car. As the words unfolded in verse, the music followed. Sometimes, I would have to quickly pull over and jot them down on whatever I could get my hands on – napkins, the inside of a book cover, a map, even on my hand so I wouldn't forget.

When I had what I thought would be the tune, I would sing it repeatedly so as not to forget it until I arrived at home. On some occasions, it did get altered, but God's message would stay in my head until the song was completed. When I arrived home, I would write the words out, then go to the keyboard and find the notes by ear, one at a time. (You see, I'm not a music writer). It is probably the strangest way to write music, but that's the way it happened for me. Good thing my memory was sharp (laugh).

Sometimes, it would be one verse and a chorus, and when I got home, I would pray about the rest of the song, and eventually, all the lyrics would be sent to me, not necessarily the same day, but usually not long after.

Other times I might be out in my kayak or walking alone on a trail. Most times, I was struggling with something in my heart, trying to cope with life itself, or unsure about my purpose in this world – mostly my purpose for God and how to bring people closer to Him.

As you read my songs, you will see the messages brought to me are not glorious, happy praises to God, but lessons for us to learn about faith, love and hope in God and His promises. He saved the glorious, happy praise songs for someone else to write. That's okay because the ones I received have been a mainstay of lessons throughout my life and kept me on track with God to pursue Peace, Love and Harmony with those I meet every day. They are a constant reminder of His love, faith and promise to us of a life eternal with Him if we follow His teachings and strive to bring others to Christ.

Of course, I love to sing His praises too and do so as often as I can. God always speaks to me in song when I most need reminders or uplifting, which is a lot in these changing times. He speaks to me through other people's music as well, and he lifts my spirits, hopes, and faith through music. Music is my best way of communicating with my Lord. I sing of Him, and He speaks to me through song.

I have often been told that I should record my music. This is a very difficult process for me; as I said previously, I am not a music writer. Although I can sing from sheet music, I can't write it. The songs are received in my head, and I play them on the guitar by ear. Then I go to the keyboard and find the notes by ear. With osteoarthritis in my hands now, I can no longer play my guitar. Thankfully, my voice is still good, and I can sing *a cappella*.

Still, as I sit through a church service or listen to someone speak of Christ and his mission, I often want to stand up right then and there and sing one of my songs the Lord sent to me because I felt His message was so important and needed to be received by all who would take time to listen. They were not meant for me alone. Of course, I didn't interrupt at the time, but because of these constant experiences, I contemplated writing a book of my songs in poetic form. After all, the words are the most important part. I still have a bucket list dream to record my songs. Music helps me, and I know others, to receive messages and keep them in our memory, which is sometimes easier than reading them. God willing, that might happen someday.

During 2020 and the COVID 19 pandemic, God had been telling me and many others to '*Be Still and Know that I Am God*,' but we weren't listening. For me, the solitude at home was initially devastating. I am a social butterfly and love to be with my grandkids, friends, and family. Being at church with my church family has always been an essential part of my life. I would go crazy staying at home.

I won't lie to you. It didn't take long for depression to set in. I tried to keep busy by cleaning, keeping in touch with people on social media, and FaceTiming with my grandkids. I made masks to help out with the pandemic, went to church online, which was okay for a while, but it wasn't the same for me. I don't do well with no contact. I am a hugger by nature. COVID-19 was killing me socially. I spent many days sitting in silence, staring into space.

I prayed to God to help me get through this. The Lord showed me Psalm 46:10 'Be Still and Know that I Am God.' I had to relax, sit back, be still, and listen for God's prompting. He would lead me in His own time.

While reading my *Daily Bread* posts and hearing others' testimonies, songs I had written kept popping up in my head, reminding me of a message from God that helped me through tough times in my life. I started to wish others could hear these words and maybe it would bring them comfort. I wished they were already out there for people to respond to, and it saddened me they were not.

Recording them didn't seem possible, especially with quarantine and social distancing happening worldwide, so as I mentioned, I decided to write a book of my songs in poetic form.

It is my hope and prayer that others in need of ministry from Jesus will be touched by His words of Faith, Encouragement, and Hope for a better future in their lives through these songs sent to me by our Lord and Saviour. This book is about lessons to keep us Strong, Hopeful, Faithful, and in appreciation of who God is and what He stands for. Each song is accompanied by a page of testimony, and a page of scriptures and quotes that harmonize with the theme of each song.

Scriptures have been taken from various bibles:

GNB Good News Bible
NRSV New Revised Standard Version
NIV New International Version

NCV   New Century Version
MSG   Message Bible
TLB   The Living Bible
NLT   New Living Translation

For some of the quotes, I used an ellipsis or paraphrased. As well, each one of my songs already has music for them.

I am still only '*Halfway There, Livin' on a Prayer*," as that song implies, but will continue as long as I am able to be in tune with our Lord and spread His messages to those who are willing to receive them. I have been so blessed by the talent the Holy Spirit has given me to speak His words through music. I encourage anyone who receives these songs of Wisdom, Faith and Assurance to pray to our Heavenly Father to help you acknowledge your talents (whatever they may be). Go forth with faith and trust in God to guide you in living your true purpose on this Earth. That is my prayer for you. Amen and Amen!!

P. S. God just helped me write this testimony. Thanks be to God!

"Hide not your talents, they for use were made,
What's a sundial in the shade?"
Benjamin Franklin

"We are all pencils in the hand of a writing God, who is sending love letters to the world."
Mother Teresa

"Give your troubles to God; He'll be up all night anyway."

"I am only one, but I am one. I cannot do everything, but I can do something, and what I should and can do with God's help I will do."

A CHILD'S LOVE

❧ TESTIMONY

God has been sending me songs since I was a young teenager. It was always in times when I most needed assurance and/or guidance. The first song I wrote was after I witnessed a young boy being physically abused by his father. He was being punished for going down the sidewalk on his tricycle away from his house. I understood him being punished, but at the same time, he was being whipped with a tree switch as his father swung him around in the air and would not stop hitting him.

It happened in front of my grandma's house, and the two of us were outside at the time and witnessed it all. My grandmother was so upset she was shaking and told the man to stop, or she would call the police. I was crying and couldn't believe what I had seen. I couldn't imagine my parents beating me like that. I felt so bad for that little boy and helpless to do anything about it.

My grandmother talked to me about it later and explained that it was unacceptable behaviour to be abusive to your child. In *Child's Love,* I wanted to express the importance of the life of a child. Children deserve to be loved and treated even better than adults because they are innocent and still growing and learning about life.

The old saying, 'A child should be seen and not heard' was definitely not part of my beliefs. Children are all precious in both God's sight and mine.

✝ SCRIPTURES TO PONDER

"I assure you that whoever does not receive the Kingdom of God like a child will never enter it."
Mark 10: 15 GNB

"Love… binds everything together in perfect harmony."
Colossians 3: 14 NRSV

❤ QUOTES

"Have a Heart that never hardens, and a Temper that never tires, and a Touch that never hurts."
Charles Dickens

"I want to help you to grow as beautiful as God meant you to be when He first thought of you."
George McDonald

"Remember your child is an independent being from you. This is his or her life.
You get to cheerlead, support and guide, but you can't make your child perform. That's up to the individual. So, take the pressure off, provide support and help, and see what happens.
Brave Writer – bravewriter.com

♫ A CHILD'S LOVE ♫

VERSE 1
A Childs love is in his eyes
Through his heart and will never die.
Find this love and hang on tight
They can help you to see the light.

VERSE 2
Why do people often say;
A child's place is far away.
Can't they see the love that shows
Come on and help him to grow.

VERSE 3
Buy his clothes, his toys, his food.
This kind of love to me is crude.
Don't they see that what he craves?
Is that special love you stored away.

VERSE 4
He needs someone when he is down.
Someone to slaughter a dreadful frown.
To take away all his miseries
And guide his soul to be free.

VERSE 5
So, listen all you people here.
Give a child's love the loudest cheer.
They deserve all of the best
For their love is the greatest gift.

A FRIEND NAMED JESUS

🕊 TESTIMONY

When I taught kids at church through girls' programs and camps (as well as Junior and Senior High camps), I always tried to impress upon them the importance of having friends. Not necessarily a lot of friends but even one good close friend, as well as the importance of having Jesus as their friend, because He is always there with you even when the others are busy or not. Most of all, I impressed on them the importance of being a good friend to others, so I wrote this song with that lesson in mind.

✝ SCRIPTURES TO PONDER

"A Friend loves you all the time, and a brother helps in times of trouble."
Proverbs 17:17 NIV

"Some Friends may ruin you, but a real Friend will be more loyal than a brother."
Proverbs 18: 24 NCV

❤ QUOTES

"I will always want you in my Life; I will always keep you in my heart…
I will always need you by my side."

"I love you not only for what you are, Lord, but for what I am when I am with You."

"My heart and soul are forever at Your service."
"A friend is the one who comes when the whole world leaves."

"What sweetness is left in life if you take away friendship? It is like robbing the world of the sun."

♫ A FRIEND NAMED JESUS ♫

VERSE 1

I've got a friend named Jesus.
I've got a friend who cares for me.
I've got a friend named Jesus, won't you come
And be His friend too.

VERSE 2

I've got a dream for Peace.
I've got a dream for Peace someday.
I've got a dream for Peace.
Won't you help me make this dream come true.

CHORUS

We and Jesus can make this dream come true.
We and Jesus can make you happy too.
We and Jesus can make Peace shine.
We can keep the world from being blind.

VERSE 3

You can have a friend named Jesus.
You can have a friend who cares for you.
You can have a friend named Jesus.
It's easy if you really try to share.

CHORUS

We and Jesus can make this dream come true.
We and Jesus can make you happy too.
We and Jesus can make Peace shine,
We can keep the world from being blind.

REPEAT VERSE 1

I've got a friend named Jesus.
I've got a friend who cares for me.
I've got a friend named Jesus.
Won't you come and be his friend too.

DREAMS FROM MORNING SUN

 TESTIMONY

I was fourteen years old when I wrote this next song, *Dreams from Morning Sun*. It was the first song I sang in front of a group of teenagers around a campfire at Junior High Camp. It was a mixed camp for girls and boys aged 12 to 14. I'm not sure how I got through it at the time because I was so nervous and scared I would mess something up on my guitar, or even worse, forget the words. But my Lord got me through the whole song perfectly.

Campfire settings became very important to me after that night, as we all sang and worshipped together. We felt at peace with God and each other. It influenced me to become a campfire director. It was my spot to be close to God, nature, and people.

This song brought me searching for God's purpose in this life. As a teenager, it was often very challenging to be a devoted Christian and still have my nonbelieving or nonpracticing friends. I felt torn on many occasions to keep my faith and try to fit in socially with others. We are so vulnerable at this stage of our lives, and I can't deny how much easier it was to follow the crowd instead of my Christian values.

I was never a delinquent person, but I also didn't share my faith. It was easier to keep that part of my life private. Even though I attended church and youth groups and enjoyed it very much, I never felt comfortable talking to nonpracticing friends about it. I know God didn't hold that against me. It was hard being a teenager.

I'm very grateful my church had a youth group I attended weekly. I had great friends and leaders I looked up to and who helped me keep my faith strong (at least on the inside, for the most part, through challenging teen years).

☦ **SCRIPTURES TO PONDER**

"My father and mother may abandon me, but the Lord will take care of me."
Psalm 27:10 NIV

"Then the King will answer, I tell you the truth, anything you did for even the least of My people here, you also did for Me."
Matthew 25: 40 NIV

❤ **QUOTES**

"I cannot change the whole world, but I can change a small part of it."
Kay Florentino

"Love is reaching, touching, and caring, sharing sunshine, flowers and hugs. So many happy hours together. Let's Be Love!"

"To live is not to live for ourselves alone; let us help one another."

"A kindness done today is the surest way to a brighter tomorrow."

♫ DREAMS FROM MORNING SUN ♫

VERSE 1

Sitting in the morning sun, dreaming of the world around me.
What visions are in my mind? I see a child crying helplessly.
Her father died from foolish mistakes.
Her mother left her because welfare wouldn't pay.

CHORUS

Dear Lord tell me, what to do. I want to help
this world any way I can.
Show me a way to make peace shine.
Throughout your promised land.
Guide me Lord, I want to lend a helping hand.

VERSE 2

Sitting in the morning sun, dreaming of the world around me.
Another vision in my mind, a girl sixteen hungry for Christs love.
Where does she turn? Her friends don't believe.
Parents don't understand and home she wants to leave.

CHORUS

Dear Lord tell me, what to do. I want to help
this world any way I can.
Show me a way to make peace shine.
Throughout your promised land.
Guide me Lord, I want to lend a helping hand.

VERSE 3

Sitting in the morning sun, dreaming of the world around me.
Still visions in my mind, I can't help but see our world ending.
How many people will be freed, how many passed by?
I can easily change that score if I just get out and try.

CHORUS
So dear Lord tell me what to do. I want to help this world
Any way I can.
Show me a way to make peace shine,
Throughout your promised land.
Guide me Lord. Let me lend a helping hand.
Sitting in the morning sun.

IN NEED

🕊 TESTIMONY

Always needing something or wanting what others have is a never satisfying circle. The more we acquire in life, the more we want, i.e., money, possessions, status, more friends. It only leads to greed and never being fulfilled.

God teaches us possessions will never bring us peace and true happiness. I, for one, am guilty of this – always trying to better myself and keep up with 'The Joneses.' I like to have nice things and keep up with the times. But I know in my heart when I reach out and share my material possessions with others or help someone get through troubled times, it brings a smile to my face and gives me 'True Peace of Mind.'

So, please be happy with what you have and be grateful to be alive. When you crave more, think of those who have much less, who need your kindness. There is always someone less fortunate than you in this world. Count your blessings and be grateful for what the Lord has given you already…LIFE!!! Someone else is fighting for theirs!

Be happy with what you have.
While working for what you want, remember, a happy and successful life Begins with God and Ends with God.
Amen

✝ SCRIPTURES TO PONDER

"God is able to bless you abundantly, so that in all things at all times, having all that you need, you will abound in every good work."
2 Corinthians 9: 8 NIV

"Isn't everything you have and everything you are sheer gifts from God?
You already have all you need."
1 Corinthians 4: 7-8 MSG

"I know what it means to be in need, and I know what it is to have plenty. I have learned the secret of being content in any and every situation whether well fed or hungry, whether living in plenty or in want. I can do all things through Christ Jesus who strengthens me."
Philippians 4: 12-13 NIV

❤ QUOTES

"Your happiness comes from within you, not from the money you make, the trips you take, or the things you own."
Faith Stewart

"To have what you want is riches, but to be able to do without is Power!"
George MacDonald

"We often take for granted the very things in life that most deserve our gratitude (air, water, soil, sun, shelter, parents, friends). Look deeper; we are so blessed."

LOVE what you have.
NEED what you want.

ACCEPT what you receive.
GIVE what you can.
Always remember: What goes around, comes around.
The Horse Mafia

♫ IN NEED ♫

VERSE 1
When you need someone, when you need a helping hand.
When you don't know where to turn and life seems close to end.
It's obvious to me, that hope you are giving up.
There's still a way you see; You've got to let your greed go free.

CHORUS
Be happy with what you have,
Be satisfied with life itself.
Turn to the Lord and you will see,
The Lord will never, ever be greedy.

VERSE 2
When you say I need this and cry when you don't receive.
When you crave for more, and no one you believe.
It's obvious to me, that life you are giving up.
There's still a way you see, you've got to let your greed go free.

CHORUS
Be happy with what you have.
Be satisfied with life itself.
Turn to the Lord, you will see,
The Lord will never, ever be greedy.

2nd CHORUS
If we live with the Lord, we will see,
There will be no more need for need.
Our lives will be free; And best of all
We'll be through with greed.
Yes, we'll be through with greed.

REMEMBERING THE PAST

🕊 TESTIMONY

I was still relatively young when I wrote this song (my late teens, I would say) and still struggling with the world and how we treat each other. I have always despised the order of society as it has been, at least in my lifetime.

Rich people are supposedly higher standing people than the middle class, and so on down the line. Possessions make you a better person than someone less fortunate. 'Not so' in my books or the Lord's.

I was bullied quite often as a young child because of my small size. And far as I could see, the ones with aggression had the most material things. They came from a higher class than I did, and I wasn't even part of the poorest in society. My family had all we needed, and sometimes extra.

It has been proven many times over the more we gain in material possessions, the more we want. True happiness is not found here. I know I am happiest when I am giving to others of my material things, time or talent, or just being there for someone who needs a hug, a listening ear, or just a friend.

Many of us, as Christians, can testify to all the great times we have had being together as a church family, sharing in fun and fellowship together. But we are not thinking of those who haven't yet begun to know the real joy we feel. The joy of acceptance for being who we are and not for what we have gained financially.

There are so many to reach out to – let's invite them to join in with us. Let's show our gratitude to our Lord and Saviour by showing how we care about others, regardless of our 'material standing in life.'

We all need each other. Rich, poor, or indifferent, we are all unique, and our hopes and dreams are much the same. We all strive for a good life on this Earth with LOVE, HOPE, JOY and PEACE. So, let's start thinking of the ones who haven't yet begun.

✝ SCRIPTURES TO PONDER

"Those who work to bring Peace are happy, because God will call them His children."
Matthew 4: 9 NIV

"Those who are treated badly for doing good are happy because the Kingdom of Heaven belongs to them."
Matthew 4: 10 NIV

❤ QUOTES

"You will find as you look back on your life that the moments when you have really lived are the moments when you have done things in the Spirit of Love."
Henry Drummond

"Lord grant that I may seek to comfort rather than to be comforted; to Love rather than be Loved."
Mother Teresa

"My greatest happiness lies in the intertwining of our dreams, hopes, hearts, and minds for each one on this earth. That we may live in harmony and peace with one another."

♫ REMEMBERING THE PAST ♫

VERSE 1

Do you remember our dreams of yesteryears?

How many times we shed such happy tears?

Do you remember how once it was said?

"Don't let your hopes get down, it's but far 'til the end."

But that was so long ago and we were so few.

Now it's time to make our dreams, tears, and hopes come true.

CHORUS

Together we had such happiness in fellowship and fun.

But we're not thinking of the ones who haven't yet begun.

VERSE 2

Do you remember how many times we prayed?

Please God be with me while I help the betrayed.

Then suddenly you find yourself turning right around,

Back into a world of fear where love has been drowned.

God has done so much for us and what does He earn?

Hate and greed and misery, His heart has been burned.

CHORUS

Together we've had such happiness in fellowship and fun.

But we're not thinking of the ones who haven't yet begun.

VERSE 3

Do you remember the stories that He shared?

Healed the sick, blind men could see; showed that He cared.

Do you remember the sacrifice He made?

Gave us everlasting life, with His own life He paid.

So, let's all take a stand for Him and show our gratitude.

Let the Lord into your heart; show Him the faith in you.

CHORUS
Together we've had such happiness in fellowship and fun.
Let's start thinking of the ones who haven't yet begun.
Yes, let's start thinking of the ones who haven't yet begun.

WHERE DO I GO TO FIND MY LORD?

 TESTIMONY

At the age of 28, I found myself divorced with two little children: a four-year-old and a six-month-old. Not a place I ever wanted to be, as having a family was at that time and still is, the most important part of my life. It was such a struggle in my 'Faith Journey' as well. All the feelings of loneliness, bitterness, and heartfelt betrayal of my husband were eating away at me. How could Jesus let this happen to me? He knew how much 'family' meant to me. I always tried to live my life in the best way possible for myself and humankind. I was always willing to help others and lend a hand. It just wasn't fair, but who said life would always be fair?

One of the hardest things I have ever had to do was hand my little children (one an infant) to another woman I did not know to look after them every other weekend. I cried many tears each time they left. We have since become friends over the many years, and I am grateful for the person she is. It could have been a much worse situation. The children were okay being with her and their dad, so that told me she was good to them. I wish many others in these situations could come to terms with the best possible scenario for the children. They are the ones who suffer the most when parents are selfish and don't put the children's feelings first.

My faith in God suffered immensely during this time. Why didn't He fix this for me? Isn't it amazing how we can believe in God and his existence in our lives when it is convenient for us, but when life takes a bad turn, He either doesn't exist, or it's all His fault!

With the love and understanding of many family members and great friends, I got through this stage in my life and thankfully realized God had been there all this time. It was me that I had to find! This song was written during that journey. I moved forward for the sake of my children and myself. God wasn't finished with me yet!

✝ SCRIPTURES TO PONDER

"I give you a new command: You must love each other as I have loved you."
John 13: 34

"Love is very patient and kind, never jealous or envious, never boastful or proud."
1 Corinthians 13: 4 TLB

❤ QUOTES

"When one door closes, another one opens; but we often look so long and regretfully at the closed door that we fail to see the one that has opened for us."
Alexander Graham Bell

"Sometimes we try prayer as a last resort when it should be our first. Thank you for Your wonderful grace Lord. That allows us to mismanage things our way, and then You not only forgive us but love us in spite of our failings."
Unknown

"Love is a fruit in season at all times and within the reach of every hand."
Mother Teresa

"GREAT opportunities to help each other seldom come, but SMALL ones
surround us daily."
Sally Koch

♪ WHERE DO I GO TO FIND MY LORD? ♪

VERSE 1

Where do I go to find my Lord?
Where do I go to find my Lord?
I could climb the highest mountain or search the widest sea.
I could ride the whirling winds of life 'til the end of eternity.

VERSE2

But after this long escapade of life is through,
Will my Lord answer me, "I love you"?
It seems so worthless when I doubt He is here.
I wonder if I'll ever understand that my Lord really cares.

VERSE3

My life seems so empty when confusions in my mind.
Is there really somewhere my Lord I will find?
People keep telling me to always pray.
They think my Lord will answer me in some very special way.

SPOKEN

You know, I think these people are so right.
I prayed, and hoped and found, that my Lord has been here all this time.
And really it was me that I had to find.

VERSE4

Now that I have found myself, confusion leaves my mind.
Got to tell this world to open eyes that are blind.
To see how my Lord loves them and what they should return.
All He asks is for love and peace and plenty of concern.
All He asks is for love and peace and plenty of concern.

BY FAITH ALONE

🕊 TESTIMONY

Although this song centres around one person who is struggling and unsure about his "Faith Journey," it also speaks to many of us about our faith in God and how we present our feelings to others searching. We each need to share our stories or testimonies and ask God to help us open our hearts to others. It is through our testimonies that people will see our strong faith in Christ. We can't make others come to Christ. They must feel that in their hearts, but by sharing our stories of how Christ was there for us in our times of need, it can show others our sincerity in our belief that God truly is there for them, too. We pray, share, and 'By Faith Alone", we leave the rest to the Lord. He gives us each our agency to follow the path we choose – good or troublesome. Choosing wisely is my prayer for all people.

☩ SCRIPTURES TO PONDER

"Try hard to live right and have faith, love and peace, together with those who trust in the Lord from pure hearts."
2 Timothy 2: 22

"Gods power protects you through your faith until salvation is shown to you at the end of time."
1 Peter 1:5

"Trust in the Lord with all thy heart, and lean not unto thine own understanding. In all thy ways acknowledge Him, and He shall 'Direct Thy Path.'"
Proverbs 3: 5-6

❤ QUOTES

"Take the first step in faith. You don't have to see the whole staircase – just take the first step."
Martin Luther King Jr.

"Little faith" will bring your soul to heaven, but "Great faith" will bring heaven to your soul!"
Charles W. Spurgeon

"We cannot force someone to hear a message they are not ready to receive, but we must never underestimate the power of "Planting a Seed."

♫ BY FAITH ALONE ♫

VERSE 1

I'll tell you a story about a friend I know.
His vision was distorted, and he doesn't know where to go.
He has so many questions about the vast unknown.
And I don't have any answers, except by faith alone.

CHORUS

By faith alone the Lord will lead me on.
My path will be directed, His message makes me strong.
"Bring forth the City of Zion", is the call we share.
We can't bring forth the City, until we start to care.

VERSE 2

My friend still has questions, I'm not getting anywhere.
Perhaps I haven't asked the Lord earnestly in prayer.
He needs to hear the stories how the Lord has helped me through,
Life's many trials and failures, but He made me stronger too.

CHORUS

By faith alone, the Lord will lead me on.
My path will be directed, His message makes me strong.
"Bring forth the City of Zion ", is the call we share.
We can't bring forth the City, until we start to care.

VERSE 3

So, I'll share my testimony and my friend will choose his way.
I'll ask the Lord please be with him, touch his heart someday.
A smile, a hug, a listening ear; I'll offer graciously.
Then I'll leave it with the Lord, His love shall set him free.

CHORUS
By faith alone, the Lord will lead me on.
My path will be directed, His message makes me strong.
"Bring forth the City of Zion", is the call we share.
We can't bring forth the City until we start to care.
No, we can't bring forth the City until we start to care.

A LITTLE LIGHT SHINES
ALL OVER THE WORLD
LOVE, HOPE, JOY AND PEACE

❧ TESTIMONY

I've done a lot of singing with kids throughout my life in many different settings.

It has brought me so much joy to watch their smiling faces singing, laughing, and feeling the spirit of the joy of the Lord shining through every one of them. Their hearts are so pure and full of love. They speak with innocence and honesty (like it or not sometimes). That has been one of my greatest gifts from the Lord. As I mentioned, campfire settings were always my favourite time to sing with kids. I have so many wonderful memories of kid's camps and directing campfire activities.

While volunteering at a school in Tobermory, Ontario, where I lived for eleven years, I was asked to teach a midday class with the children. I called it *The Friendship Club.* The kids signed up voluntarily to take turns coming along. We started this club so kids would try to get along better at recess times. They were really struggling with this. I focused on sharing, caring, respect for each other and recognizing their differences, and especially not bullying. The class went very well, and the kids were always eager to join in. We did skits, made friendship crafts to hand out to others at school. And of course, sang lots of songs with actions and laughter.

Some of the songs I wrote or altered from other songs when I wasn't able to use 'Christian words' in the school setting (which I procrastinated about). The kids were willing to share their feelings and discuss things happening on the playground. We would act them out and choose a better solution. They always had the right answers. They just needed to learn to voice their feelings with some guidance in handling their emotions in times of stress or confrontation. Kids are awesome!

The next three songs are ones I wrote mostly for children.

✟ SCRIPTURES TO PONDER – A Little Light Shines

"Your word is like a lamp unto my feet, and a light unto my path."
Psalm 119: 105

"Allow the light of the Lord into your heart. For the light of our Saviour brings true life! Transform yourself!"
John 8:12

"Jesus talked to the people saying, 'I am the light of the world. The person who follows me will never live in darkness, but will have the light that gives life.'"
John 8:12

❤ QUOTES

"There are two ways of spreading light: to be the candle or the mirror that reflects it."
Edith Wharton

"A smile happens in a flash, but the memory of it can last a lifetime."

Let your light so shine.
It is in the darkest of times that the tiniest light can make the biggest difference.
What is our light?
It is the energy of our personal existence.
Some light the world with their smiles,
Some with their love.
Some light the world with caring.
While others shine with knowledge.
Each of us was given a special light with a purpose.
Help us to "Boldly Shine" as You intended, Lord.
Amen

♫ A LITTLE LIGHT SHINES ♫

VERSE1

There's a little light shining from the sun today,
There's a little light shining from the sun today.
There's a little light shining from the sun today.
Praise the Lord!

VERSE 2

There's a little light shining from the stars at night.
There's a little light shining from the stars at night.
There's a little light shining from the stars at night.
Praise the Lord!

VERSE 3

Keep a little light shining from your heart each day.
Keep a little light shining from your heart each day.
Keep a little light shining from your heart each day.
Praise the Lord! Praise the Lord! PRAISE THE LORD!

✝ SCRIPTURES TO PONDER –
All Over the World

"I have told you these things so that you can have joy, I have so that your joy will be the fullest possible joy!"
John 15: 11

"Let the peace that Christ gives control your thinking because you were all called together in one body to have peace."
Colossians 3:15

"Prepare your minds for service and have self-control.
All your hope should be for the gift of grace that will be yours when Jesus Christ is shown to you."
1 Peter 1:13

♥ QUOTES

"Keep your face to the sunshine, and you cannot see the shadow"

"Love looks not with the eyes but with the heart!"
Shakespeare

"Lord, may I seek to comfort rather than be comforted. Seek to love than to be loved."

♫ All Over the World ♫

VERSE 1

Spread a lot of sunshine all over the world.
Spread a lot of sunshine all over the world.
Spread it far, spread it wide,
Spread it straight up to the sky.
Spread a lot of sunshine all over the world.

VERSE 2

Spread a lot of Love all over the world.
Spread a lot of Love all over the world.
Spread it far, spread it wide,
Spread it straight up to the sky.
Spread a lot of Love all over the world.

VERSE 3

Spread a lot of Joy all over the world.

VERSE 4

Spread a lot of Peace all over the world.

VERSE 5

Spread a lot of Hope all over the world.

This is an action song for kids.

✟ SCRIPTURES TO PONDER –
Love, Hope, Joy and Peace

"These three remain: Faith, Hope and Love. But the greatest of these is Love.
Follow the way of Love."
1 Corinthians 13: 13, 14:1 NIV

"He will yet fill your mouth with laughter and your lips with shouts of joy."
Job 8:21 NIV

"May the God of Hope fill you with Joy and Peace as you trust in Him; so that you may overflow with Hope by the power of the Holy Spirit."
Romans 15: 13 NIV

❤ QUOTES

"May the Joy that lives in our hearts today be our song of love for a million tomorrows of peace."
Unknown

"Two persons cannot long be friends if they cannot forgive each other's mistakes."

"Love looks not with the eyes but with the heart."

♫ Love, Hope, Joy and Peace ♫

VERSE 1

Communities of Love, Hope, Joy and Peace,
Love, Hope, Joy and Peace,
Love, Hope, Joy and Peace.
Communities of Love, Hope, Joy and Peace,
Are growing everywhere.

VERSE 2

So many need Love, Hope, Joy and Peace.
Love, Hope, Joy and Peace.
Love, Hope, Joy and Peace.
So many need Love, Hope, Joy and Peace,
For the Lord will soon be here.

VERSE 3

God gives us all Love, Hope, Joy and Peace,
Love, Hope, Joy and Peace.
Love, Hope, Joy and Peace.
God gives us all Love, Hope, Joy and Peace,
Through His Son who really cares.

VERSE 4

Sing out your songs of Love, Hope, Joy and Peace.
Love, Hope, Joy and Peace.
Love, Hope, Joy and Peace.
Sing out your songs of Love, Hope, Joy and Peace,
To all the people everywhere.

PEACE

🕊 **TESTIMONY**

Living in a world of deep unrest can tax us all, even in the best of times. Wars, famine, isolation, and sickness weigh heavy on our hearts. It is sometimes mind-boggling to know how we can make a difference in this world. But still, God summons us to make peace, keep peace, live peace – JUST BE PEACE!

We can't do everything, but we can do something!

☩ SCRIPTURES TO PONDER

"Live in harmony and peace. And may the God of love and peace be with you."
2 Corinthians 13:11 TLB

"Do what you learned and received from Me, what I told you, and what you saw Me do. And the God who gives peace will be with you."
Philippians 4:9 NCV

"I leave you peace. My peace I give you. I do not give it to you as the world does. So, don't let your hearts be troubled or afraid. You heard Me say to you; I am going, but I am coming back to you."
John 14: 27 & 28

"May the Lord bless you and keep you. May the Lord show you His kindness and have mercy on you. May the Lord watch over you and give you peace."
Numbers 5: 24-26 NCV

❤ QUOTES

"The seed of joy grows best in a field of peace."
Robert J. Wicks

"A friend should be loved freely for himself and not for anything else. A friend is a gift you give yourself. Do good to the friend to keep him, to thy enemy to gain him."

♫ PEACE ♫

CHORUS

Peace to you my friends
Peace to you is my goal.
Peace to you from heaven above.
Let peace stay in your soul.

VERSE 1

Peace is a word you can freely give.
Peace is a word from the Lord.
Peace from Lennon, King and more.
Peace is a worldwide chord.

CHORUS

Peace to you my friends.
Peace to you is my goal.
Peace to you from heaven above.
Let peace stay in your soul.

VERSE 2

Peace says it all in the smile you give.
Peace is the food that we share.
Peace is your time given freely too,
Find peace in a world of fear.

CHORUS

Peace to you my friends.
Peace to you is my goal.
Peace to you from heaven above.
Let peace stay in your soul.

VERSE 3

Peace from the cross where His head hung low.
Peace through the words that He shared.

Peace we'll receive when we spread His news.
That Jesus the Christ is King.

CHORUS
Peace to you my friends.
Peace to you is my goal.
Peace to you from heaven above.
Let Peace stay in your soul.

YOU ARE THE VINE

 ## TESTIMONY

When I lived in Tobermory, I would often go off in my kayak on Dorcas Bay, which was right on our property's shoreline. I needed alone time to be with God.

In the quietness of one of my excursions, I felt these words come to me in song, talking to me about nature and how it all fits in with our Heavenly Father and His vast creations given freely for us to enjoy.

I asked God to plant my roots deep in faith and guide me in planting new seeds so others would come to learn of his ways. I prayed that I might help bring peace to them the same way He brought it to me. Just knowing He was close by all the time for each of us.

No matter how lonely you may feel, push yourself to reach out to your Heavenly Father. He will guide your way. You only need to ask. Look for someone who could use your help or guidance. There is always someone less fortunate than you or who needs a shoulder to cry on or someone to listen. You don't have to do anything "great or triumphant." Just be there. Count your blessings and share your time with others. God will bless you for it, and you will feel needed, which we all want to feel sometimes. Being needed helps to get rid of our selfish, 'poor me' thoughts that are not good for any of us. Try it. You'll see!

Amen

✝ SCRIPTURES TO PONDER

"I am the vine, and you are the branches. If any remain in Me and I remain in them, they produce much fruit. But without Me they can do nothing."
John 15:5 NIV

❤ QUOTES

"The reason birds can fly and we can't is simply that they have perfect faith, for to have faith is to have wings."
J.M. Barrie

"Here is the test to find out whether your mission on earth is finished: If you're alive, IT ISN'T!"
Richard Bach

"You are part of a great plan, an indispensable part. You are needed; you have your own unique share in the freedom of creation."
Madeleine L'Engle

"Stand tall and proud of who you are and the journey you've had. Go out on a limb by facing your fears and challenge yourself. Remember your roots; they are deep. Plant your roots deep in faith! Be content with life itself. Enjoy the view!"
Unknown

♫ YOU ARE THE VINE ♫

CHORUS
You are the vine of the earth my Lord.
Am I a branch that You need?
Send all Your words on wings of love.
Plant my roots deep in faith.

VERSE 1
I hear the birds in the trees, My Lord.
Their songs are the sounds of new spring.
Reminding us all of what new life holds.
The promise of love that you bring.

VERSE 2
I see the stars in the sky, my Lord.
They light all the heavens you've made.
Each one has a story to share with us,
As we enter Your kingdom someday.
CHORUS
You are the vine of the Earth, my Lord.
Am I a branch that you need?
Send all your words on wings of love.
Plant my roots deep in faith.

VERSE 3
Teach us to plant new seeds my Lord.
So, others may learn of your ways.
Bring peace to them as you've brought it to me.
This shall be my prayer every day.
CHORUS
You are the vine of the earth, my Lord.
Am I a branch that you need?
Send all your words on wings of love.
Plant my roots deep in faith.
Plant my roots deep in faith.

I'M ALWAYS WITH YOU

🕊 TESTIMONY

When my husband and I moved to Tobermory, I left behind family, friends, and my church life which has always been so important. I didn't realize at the time how difficult this transition would be for me. It seemed like a great adventure at the time –a stunning countryside on the Bruce Peninsula with lots of fresh air.

We lived in a beautiful new home my husband built overlooking Dorcas Bay. We were in 'God's Country,' as many of our visitors would say to us. We had a variety of guests because we started a Bed and Breakfast business. In all this beauty and fresh air, I was still missing my family and church family. My church back home didn't have a congregation in our area.

Somewhere in my loneliness, God sent me this song. I began attending a local United Church. It wasn't easy for me at first to fit in with all new people. Not that they weren't kind, because they were, it was just different than what I was used to. Their services were different, yet somewhat the same. We can get so caught up in our own traditions that we fail to see goodness in others.

I soon realized these people's dreams were much the same as mine. We all had love for God and man, and we all wanted to be needed doing what we could to help others in need.

I was asked to share my songs at their services, and over time made many new friends. It became my home away from home. This song still speaks to me. It is a constant reminder for me that God is always with me!

Thanks be to God!

✝ SCRIPTURES TO PONDER

"Have I not commanded you? Be strong and courageous. Do not be afraid; do not be discouraged, for the Lord your God will be with you wherever you go."
Joshua 1: 9 NIV

"When you face trials, God will be with you. You are not alone. When you go through "Deep Water," I will be with you. When you go through "Rivers of Difficulty," you will not drown."
Isaiah 43:2 NIV

"Don't be afraid, for I am with you. Don't be dismayed, for I am your God. I will strengthen you. Yes, I will help you. Yes, I will uphold you with the right hand of My righteousness."
Isaiah 41: 10

❤ QUOTES

"No matter how many miles there might be between us, we can always touch the ones we love."
Unknown

"What you achieve through the journey of life is not as important as who you become."
Unknown

"How blessed am I that I can walk beside You, lean upon You, and live within the warmth of Your love."
Roy Lessin

♫ I'M ALWAYS WITH YOU ♫

CHORUS

I'm always with you, when you're far away from home.
I'm always with you, no matter where you roam.
I'm always with you, just put your trust in me.
I'm always with you; Faith is the key!

VERSE 1

We travel many roads in life, and always come around,
To places where are hearts are kept; no matter where we're bound.
We seem to find a solace there; that words cannot explain.
Why can't we feel it everywhere, is not each place the same?

VERSE 2

We see the same surroundings, take on a different look.
But our homes, schools and churches, all match the storybooks.
And people's dreams are much the same, no matter where we live.
And I have promised many things, if you will only give.

CHORUS

I'm always with you, when you're far away from home.
I'm always with you, no matter where you roam.
I'm always with you, just put your trust in Me.
I'm always with you, Faith is the key.

VERSE 3

We need to see the Love of God in other places too.
They hold the same gifts we have; the ones God gave to you.
He gave His Love to us in trust; in faith we need to share.
Fly high My child I'm with you, forever I'll be there.

CHORUS
I'm always with you, when you're far away from home.
I'm always with you, no matter where you roam.
I'm always with you, just put your trust in Me.
I'm always with you, Faith is the key.
Faith is the key! I'm always with you.

BE STILL AND KNOW

🕊 TESTIMONY

A couple of years ago, God started putting a Bible verse in front of me. It happened quite often, and I started seeing it everywhere. It was on mugs, T-shirts, candles, blocks of wood – literally everywhere. It was familiar to me in scripture already, but suddenly, God was pointing it out to me. *Be Still and Know that I Am God* (Psalm 46:10). I had written a song called 'Be Still and Know' before this happened. The song meant a lot to me, of course, because God was telling me again He was here for me and I needed to slow down, get quiet and listen for His still, small voice. It wasn't until a particular September, when I attended a Woman's Retreat at one of our church campgrounds, that I realized just how important this song would be to me.

A dear friend of mine and I were one of about ninety women at this retreat.

The experience I'm about to share brought many of us closer to God that weekend. Another lady who I did not know before the retreat had placed a gift on the penny sale table. It was a candle with a block of wood beside it. On the block was the Scripture *Be Still and Know*. When I saw it there, I told my friend I wanted to win this prize because of the song I wrote and because I felt God was telling me something once again. I told her if I won it, I would sing the song in the talent show that evening (even though I was recuperating from thyroid surgery, which affected my voice box temporarily). What was I thinking!

Well, I won the gift! My friend looked at me in surprise and said, "I guess you have to sing it now. I went to the talent show coordinator and told her my story. She said, "Yes, you have to sing it." I told her it was a serious song and could she place it in the latter part of the program. Little did I know she placed me as the 'Grand Finale.' I was terrified. How was I going to pull this off? I had no music. The song was just in my head. I couldn't play guitar because of my hands. I would have to sing it *a cappella*. It was the final song of a so-far fantastic talent show.

I got up, shared my experience, and asked for everyone's prayers to help me get through it. I knew it needed to be shared. By the time I was finished singing, my lips were literally sticking together. I had no moisture left in my mouth, but every word came out as clear and on key as could be. Everyone stood up and applauded. I said, "Thank you, Lord. That wouldn't have come out without you." I'll be careful about what I promise in the future.

There were so many testimonies shared at our closing service the next morning. I knew, as did the other lady who brought the gift, that God was working through us that weekend. God had prompted her weeks before to bring that gift to the retreat. She was also struggling with her "Faith Journey," as many of us were.

Another woman shared that she didn't understand what was happening here, but she never felt this feeling of togetherness before in her entire life. It was her first time at a retreat such as this. I had not been to one in many years. God had witnessed to her, and most of the ninety women at this retreat through myself and another woman's testimony. It was truly a spiritual feeling of oneness in Christ. 'God works in mysterious ways' was an understatement that weekend.

"Be Still and Know that He is God."

Amen

✝ SCRIPTURES TO PONDER

"For I know the plans I have for you," declares the Lord. "Plans to prosper you and not harm you; plans to give you hope and a future."
Jeremiah 29:11 NIV

"Be Still and know that I am God."
Psalm 46:10

"The Lord will fight for you; you need only to be Still."
Exodus 14:14

"My presence will go with you, and I will give you rest."
Exodus 33: 14 NIV

❤ QUOTES

"All of my wishes and all of my dreams are beginning to come true through you."

"What if your struggle is simply God's way of saying, "I miss you." It's time to slow down and go to the Father and lay your burdens down at his feet. No more running from God. No more trying to fight by yourself. No more trying to please man. Just you and God together."

"Love each other warmly, with all your hearts."

"Wait in faith. Everything God has promised is coming. And His timing is perfect."
Dr. James McDonald

♪ BE STILL AND KNOW ♪

VERSE 1

Be still and know that I am God.

Be still; let Jesus in your heart.

Be still; reach down to your soul.

Be still; and let go.

CHORUS

For I am your Lord, and I'll be here by your side.

For I am your Lord, in your heart I will abide.

For I am your Lord, and I'll teach you My will.

Please let go and be still,

Please let go and be still.

VERSE 2

Be still and know that I am God.

Be still; pray for those who need your prayers.

Be still; don't be afraid to love,

My child, I'm watching from above.

CHORUS

For I am your Lord, and I'll be here by your side.

For I am your Lord, in your heart I will abide.

For I am your Lord, and I'll teach you My will.

Please let go and be still,

Please let go and be still.

VERSE 3

Be still and know that I am God.

Be still; hold tight to your faith.

Be still; My promise you'll see.

Your hopes and dreams shall come alive through Me.

CHORUS
For I am your Lord, and I'll be here by your side.
For I am your Lord, in your heart I will abide.
For I am your Lord, and I'll teach you my will.
Please let go and be still. Please let go and be still.

BEEN A LONG TIME LORD

 TESTIMONY

Sometimes we just get caught up with life itself, and although we know that God is with us, we can take Him for granted in the busyness of everyday living. Although we have our own lives to live, we tend to put God and His work for us on this Earth on the back burner, making excuses about having no time left in a day for others. We barely have time to accomplish our own tasks, and God soon gets forgotten.

God soon let me know this was happening in my journey. He sent me this song to remind me to put Him back in the foreground. I needed to start doing what He called me to do – work for Him.

Not long after I wrote this song, I was called to be a minister in my church. I readily accepted the call.

Praise be to God!

✝ SCRIPTURES TO PONDER

"He said, 'The right time has come. The kingdom of God is near. Change your hearts and lives and believe the Good News!'"

"The joy of the Lord is your strength!"
Nehemiah 8: 10 NLT

"The Lord says, 'Even now, come back to me with all your heart. Go without food, and cry and be sad.' Let your heart be broken. Come back to the Lord your God."
Joel 2: 12 & 13 NCV

❤ QUOTES

"How to Fix the World – put Jesus back in all the places you asked Him to leave – home, school, government, church, and most of all, 'Your Heart.'"

"My heart holds the sound of your voice and the soft brightness which is your soul."
Unknown

"Every day I realize how much I love You, Lord, and how much it means to me to know that You are there… to share in all the moments of my life."
Unknown

♫ BEEN A LONG TIME LORD ♫

VERSE 1

It's been a long time Lord; since I felt You in my heart.
It's been a long time Lord; and I really don't want to part.
It's been a long time Lord; bring me back where I should be.
It's been as long time Lord; reach me, teach me.

VERSE 2

It's been a long time Lord; I know I have work to do.
It's been a long time Lord; I can't make it without You.
It's been a long time Lord; be my strength, be my guide.
It's been a long time Lord; place Jesus by my side.

VERSE 3

Give me another chance Lord; to do what you want me to do.
Give me another chance Lord; and I'll always have faith in you.
Give me another chance Lord; I'll not waste any more time.
Give me another chance Lord; use me and we'll make peace shine.

VERSE 4

It's been a long time Lord; since I felt You in my heart.
It's been a long time Lord; and I really don't want to part.
Give me another chance Lord; bring me back where I should be.
Give me another chance Lord; reach me, teach me.

BABY GIRL

 TESTIMONY

When my daughter was about to get married, I was living six hours away in Tobermory. It had always been a struggle for me not to be close to my family, especially my kids. Whenever they did have time to make the journey for a visit, it was always bittersweet. I was so happy to see them and spend time with them. But when it was time for them to leave and go back to their home, I was so sad that I cried watching them head out the driveway, knowing it would be some time until I saw them again. I would always go into a depression for a while.

As time got closer to the wedding day, I pondered how I could make this day extra special for my daughter (other than the usual things a mom does for the bride).

I decided to write a song in her honour. I have always been so very proud of both my son and daughter.

When the wedding day arrived, I had already decided not to sing the song for her at the reception. It was her day, and I didn't want to stand out and take attention away from her. So, when it was time to do my 'Mother's Speech,' I simply recited her song to her. It was a very moving experience for me. The song said what was in my heart.

No greater love on Earth do I have than the love of my children, and now, my grandchildren. I am so blessed!

✝ SCRIPTURES TO PONDER

"Love is patient and kind, Love is not jealous, it does not brag, and it is not proud. Love is not rude, is not selfish, and does not get upset with others."
1 Corinthians 13: 4 & 5 NCV

♥ QUOTES

"I never thought I'd find a love so strong and true, a love that covers every fault, a love each day made new."
Mark Batso

"The most precious jewels you will ever have around your neck are the arms of your children."
Unknown

"When God gave you to me, it was as if He… planted the image of you deep in my heart… there to remain forever beautiful and cherished."
Roy Lessin

"I promise to give you all my love for now and forever, to keep your love close to my heart so that we will never grow apart."

My Child…
"Never forget how much I love you. As you grow older, you will face many challenges in life; just do your best. I might not be with you, but know I believe in you. You were, and always will be, the best thing that ever happened to me."
- Mom

♫ BABY GIRL ♫

VERSE 1

The day you came into my life, I was truly blessed.
Your tiny hands touched mine alone, it took away my breath.
And in those precious moments, I knew that I would be,
The one to guide and teach you, life's many mysteries.

CHORUS

Baby girl; you're a wonder to behold.
You gave my life new meaning, as you reached down to my soul.
Baby girl; I hope that I have been
The mother you're deserving of; a friend to share your dreams.

VERSE 2

You grew into a little girl, with eyes blue as the sky.
You touched the hearts of many, and I need not wonder why.
Friends you were to all you met; you never left one behind.
You always gave your very best; how proud I was you're mine.

CHORUS

Baby girl; you're a wonder to behold.
You gave my life new meaning, as you reached down to my soul.
Baby girl; I hope that I have been
The mother your deserving of; a friend to share your dreams.

VERSE 3

And now your childhood days are gone, a bride you soon will be.
Someone came into your life, so I'll have to set you free.
Someday I hope that you will have a precious moment too,
When tiny hands touch yours alone, a miracle for you.

CHORUS

Baby girl; you're a wonder to behold.
You gave my life new meaning, as you reached down to my soul.
Baby girl; I hope that I have been
The mother you're deserving of; a friend to share your dreams.

END OF THE ROAD

 TESTIMONY

This song speaks to me about the end of our journey on this Earth and how our life's possessions are meaningless in the scheme of things when we reach the end.

I have never believed that life is ever over for us. We will be somewhere. Whether it be in a glorious life with our Heavenly Father or a place of much sadness and hatred – it is our choice. God gives us that right to choose.

Sometimes when family members or people close to us pass to this new beginning in the afterlife, we have genuine concerns about where they will end up. In some cases, it's hard to deal with what we feel will be their destination. But we know the Lord loves every one of us, and each one's judgment will be different from the next person. We are all accountable in our unique way.

We are not the judge nor the jury. Let's worry about ourselves and how we live our lives, leaving the rest to God. He knows all about every one of us and will make the call.

How do you choose to live at the end of your journey on this earth? "Your Choice"!!

I'm going to continue Walking by Faith, travelling my road, doing what I can for others, and praying God will take my hand and lead me home to a peaceful ever after.

Amen

✝ SCRIPTURES TO PONDER

"Because of Christ and our faith in Him, we can now come boldly and confidently into God's presence."
Ephesians 3: 12 NLT

"Whosoever believeth in Him should not perish, but have everlasting life."
John 3:16 NLT

"Your gold and silver is cankered; and the rust of them shall be a witness against you."
James 5:3 KIV

❤ QUOTES

"The way is long- let us go together."
"The way is difficult- let us help each other."
"The way is joyful- let us share it."
"The way is ours alone- let us go in love."
Unknown

"Looking back on all that we've shared and all that is yet to come, I realize that nothing life may offer me could make me happier than a future in Eternity with You Lord."
Unknown

"Still round the corner there may wait. A new road, or a secret gate."
J.R.R. Tolkien

♫ END OF THE ROAD ♫

VERSE 1

There is a light at the end of the road.
A shining light, no silver or gold.
And through this light Jesus will bring me home.
To be with You Lord at the end of the road.

VERSE 2

How shall we get there to the end of that road?
Have we forgot that Jesus made us whole?
He bled and died so we could see that light.
Everlasting life at the end of the road.

VERSE 3

My dreams live on past the end of the road.
Love, joy and hopes will finally be foretold.
All nations one, all families, friends and foe.
Shall live in peace at the end of the road.

VERSE 4

So, let's walk in faith as we travel down that road.
We'll leave behind all our silver and gold.
Walk hand in hand with Jesus will go on,
To meet with You Lord at the end of the road.

We'll meet with You Lord at the end of the road.
With everlasting life at the end of the road.
We'll live in peace at the end of the road.

SACRED GROUNDS

 TESTIMONY

The church I am a member of has ownership of campgrounds in many unique settings worldwide. We call these camps 'Our Reunion Grounds.' For decades, we met annually at our campgrounds in our local regions. Sometimes, we visited camps in other areas as well and shared a week-long camping experience with those folks. We gathered together as a church family (sometimes friends come along as well) to share in a time of learning, reminiscing, praying, worshipping our Lord and renewing and strengthening our relationship with our Heavenly Father.

These special grounds became a 'Sacred Place' in our hearts for many of us over the years spent attending camp. Many great memories were shared, new friends were made, and old friends reunited. We laughed, joked, told stories, and even cried tears. Even though our geographical areas are different, the memories are much the same – but also unique and some very spiritual. Each time we met, our purpose was the same. To leave refreshed in spirit, to go back to our everyday life and spread Joy, Hope, Love and Peace to those who are willing to listen.

Due to COVID-19, we were not able to meet at any of our camps. It has been very difficult for all of us who attend, especially the children, who look forward to renewing friendships, swimming, and especially campfire – my favourite time.

I spent a lot of time there alone this summer, walking the beach and reminiscing about times past. I decided to write this song in memory of the campgrounds we have shared over the years.

Thank you, Lord, for giving us these 'Sacred Grounds.' They have given so much love to so many. My prayer is that we always share our camp experiences with others and open our arms to them with an invitation to join in.

Amen

✞ SCRIPTURES TO PONDER

"We were all called together in one body to have peace.

Look around you. People are gathering and coming to you. Your sons are coming from far away and your daughters are coming with them. When you see them, you will shine with happiness; you will be excited and full of joy."
Isaiah 60: 4 & 5 NCV

"The group of believers were united in their hearts and spirits. All those in the group acted as though their private property belonged to everyone in the group. In fact, they shared everything."
Acts 4: 32 NCV

"There is a time to cry and a time to laugh.
There is a time to be sad and a time to dance.
There is a time to throw away stones and a time to gather them.
There is a time to hug and a time not to hug."
Ecclesiastes 3: 4 & 5 NCV

❤ QUOTES

"In the circle, we are all equal. There is no one in front of you. And there is nobody behind you. No one is above you; No one is below you. The circle is sacred because it is designed to create unity."
LAKOTA WISDOM

♫ SACRED GROUNDS ♫

VERSE 1

How can I explain, the feelings that You gave us?
How can I explain, all the memories we've shared?
You gave us peace and love, Hopes and dreams for tomorrow,
As we worshipped You on these Sacred Grounds.

CHORUS

How blessed we've been each time; we've shared each other's journey.
How blessed we've been to know; Lord You've been here by our side.
Teach us now to share all the memories we've witnessed.
When we speak the name of these Sacred Grounds.

VERSE 2

Families and friends have fellowshipped together.
Witnessing Baptisms, through sunshine and rain.
You calmed the storms around, brought tears of joy among us.
Sharing sacraments on these Sacred Grounds.

VERSE 3

Sitting peaceful on the beach, with campfire blazing.
We laughed and sang the songs; our spirits rose so high.
You touched our hearts with hugs, and gave our lives new meaning.
Again, we worshipped You on these Sacred Grounds.

CHORUS

How blessed we've been each time; we've shared each other's journey.
How blessed we've been to know; Lord You've been here by our side.
Teach us now to share all the memories we've witnessed.
When we speak the name of these Sacred Grounds.

VERSE 4

The years have passed us by, many changes we have seen here.
The buildings, trees and shore have taken all its toll.
But the history we've made will never be forgotten.
If we share our love of these Sacred Grounds.

VERSE 5

Thankyou Lord above for giving us this treasure.
We have been so richly blessed, never could we repay,
For all the special times and memories we've shared here.
As we've worshipped you on these Sacred Grounds.

CHORUS

How blessed we've been each time we shared each other's journey.
How blessed we've been to know; Lord You've been here by our side.
Teach us now to share all the memories we've witnessed.
When we speak the name of these Sacred Grounds,
When we speak the name of these Sacred Grounds.

CONCLUSION

Thoughts to send you forth on your Life's Journey.

God is still writing your life's story. Quit trying to steal the pen. Trust the Author.

Don't try to rush God's plan for your life. Everything will happen exactly when it is supposed to. Have Patience, Faith and never stop Believing!

"As Christ's Lordship enlarges to cover every area of your life, you will find the peace, joy, and freedom He promises to His followers. It's guaranteed!"
Debra Evans, Kindred Hearts

Heavenly Father,
Today, I pray you use me to impact others. Purpose my encounters with others to be full of meaning and opportunity. Open up the door for me to show Your love and reveal Your truth to someone today. My heart's desire, Lord, is for people to come to know You. Use me today to reach out to those who are without You or to those who walked away from You. Give me the confidence to purpose my words and actions, and whisper into my heart when the opportunity presents itself. In Jesus's name, *Amen.*

May your faith in the Lord be strengthened with songs of Love, Hope, Joy and Peace is my prayer.

www.ingramcontent.com/pod-product-compliance
Lightning Source LLC
Chambersburg PA
CBHW061039050726
47592CB00004B/1515